Original title:
The Truth About Life's Meaning (Spoiler: There Is None)

Copyright © 2025 Creative Arts Management OÜ
All rights reserved.

Author: Miriam Kensington
ISBN HARDBACK: 978-1-80566-289-1
ISBN PAPERBACK: 978-1-80566-584-7

Invisible Threads Weaving Stories

In a world of mismatched socks,
We search for meaning in the blocks.
A riddle wrapped in a taco shell,
Life laughs, and we just can't tell.

We juggle dreams like clumsy clowns,
With smirks of fate, we wear our frowns.
Wormholes pop in a bowl of stew,
Yet here we dance, just me and you.

In a game of chess with no one there,
We sip our tea, without a care.
The cat is king, the dog our knight,
In cosmic jest, we take our flight.

So let's toast to the absurd parade,
Where questions linger, yet answers fade.
With laughter bright, we'll sail the stream,
For in this jest, we find our theme.

An Odyssey Through the Void

Once a sailor lost at sea,
With a compass pointing to what's free.
A map that's just a doodle line,
We'll find our way, it's just divine!

The stars above, they roll their eyes,
As we debate if pizza flies.
With every wave, we laugh and sway,
In this vast nothing, we'll find a way.

On a raft made of cereal boxes,
We dodge the doubts like clever foxes.
Reality is a game of charades,
Yet here we are, making parades.

So grab your hat and never fret,
Life is a dance, don't you forget.
With skits and jokes, we'll claim our share,
In this void, we're fabulously rare.

Beneath the Weight of the Infinite

A hamster spins its wheel of fate,
While pondering if dessert arrives late.
In a universe of bloated dreams,
We sip on chaos, or so it seems.

With butterflies debating the laws,
Of gravity and snoring bears' claws.
We chase our tails, we run in place,
A fickle smile on nature's face.

In the grand bazaar of cosmic jest,
The chicken crossed the road with zest.
To find the punchline at the end,
Where meaning morphs, just like a friend.

So let's not stress on heavy sighs,
For life's just one of many tries.
With giggles soft and hearts so bold,
In this wild tale, let's break the mold.

Whispers of the Void

In the cosmos where we dwell,
Stars giggle as they fell.
Wormholes tease the clueless mind,
Answers lost, nowhere to find.

Life's a puzzle, missing pieces,
While reality just sneezes.
Chasing shadows, trying to glean,
What it all could really mean.

Dancing atoms, playing charades,
Hoping fate won't wear our shades.
Awake we are, yet sleep we crave,
In this circus, are we brave?

So pour a drink, let's toast the void,
Existence's jokes, we are employed.
For laughter's light, with all its quirks,
Makes sense of our senseless perks.

Fragments of a Fragmented Soul

Pieces scattered, glued with dreams,
Life's a riddle, bursting seams.
Thoughts collide in traffic jams,
Questions wrapped in silly prams.

Once I tried to chart my fate,
But numbers laughed, called it a date.
Maps drawn by a drunken king,
Showed me more of everything.

Mirror, mirror, on the wall,
Who's the silliest of them all?
Reflections wink and play along,
Hum a tune of freedom's song.

So let's embrace the wild absurd,
While pigeons plot and vision's blurred.
Life is fruitless, but we find,
Joy in madness, bliss aligned.

Echoes in an Empty Universe

In a vacuum where echoes sway,
Laughter drifts, then slips away.
Galaxies spin, all in jest,
Life's a quiz, but who can guess?

Stars twinkle like they know the score,
But they're just light, nothing more.
A pizza slice, a cosmic pie,
Served with sarcasm, oh me, oh my!

Comets streak with tails of glee,
Winks of fate, are we just free?
Gravity, it pulls but lets us roam,
In this vast and empty dome.

So let's raise a glass to cosmic cheer,
To nothingness that feels so near.
For in this giggle, voids collude,
Life is silly, nothing to conclude.

A Journey Without a Destination

We wander roads that lead nowhere,
With maps that laugh, we're full of flair.
In circles, round we skip and prance,
Chasing shadows in a silly dance.

Each step we take is quite absurd,
Life's the joke, we are the bird.
With every turn, we lose the plot,
Yet somehow find joy in the not.

Reflections in a Shattered Mirror

A broken glass, oh what a sight,
Myself in pieces, left and right.
I smile at fractures, chuckle with glee,
Who knew chaos could set us free?

Each shard reveals a different face,
A funhouse game, this silly space.
I wave to my pieces, they wave back,
As we embrace the quirky track.

The Chorus of Uncertainty

In life's big show, applause is rare,
The script is blank, we're unaware.
We dance and sing without a clue,
Making up tunes as we pass through.

The notes are flat, the rhythm's off,
Yet still we laugh; we just can't scoff.
A band of misfits, loud and free,
In the symphony of absurdity.

Ephemeral Echoes of Being

Life's a flash, a fleeting glance,
A spark, a giggle, a clumsy dance.
We come, we go, like passing trains,
Leaving behind our goofy stains.

In laughter's wake, we leave our mark,
Like fireflies glowing in the dark.
With moments brief, we find delight,
In the silly shadows of the night.

Wandering Without a Map

I'm lost but that's just fine,
A wrong turn is still divine.
With every step, I have a laugh,
Who needs a map? I choose a path.

Each friend says, "You'll find the way!"
I grin and think, "What's a cliché?"
In fields where wildflowers creep,
I chase a thought, then fall asleep.

Beneath the Facade of Clarity

I wore my glasses, thought I'd see,
But all they brought was mockery.
A bright sunbeam, it seemed so clear,
Yet even shadows laugh with cheer.

The clock ticks loud, a silly game,
Yet all I hear is my own name.
I search for answers in my tea,
But it just brews absurdity.

The Unraveling of Tomorrow

Tomorrow knocks with a silly grin,
Says, "Why fret? Let chaos begin!"
I try to plan, but plans like to flee,
Like socks in the wash, it's a mystery.

With every dawn, a new surprise,
Some mundane, some with sparkly eyes.
Juggling dreams like eggs, I fall,
And laugh it off, what's the call?

Fragments of Unfulfilled Wishes

Wishes scattered like confetti,
In a carnival that's not quite ready.
I pick them up, then toss in the breeze,
A joke, a giggle, if you please.

With hope balloons that float away,
I'll tie them down for just one day.
Fragments shimmer, all out of reach,
But even broken bits can teach.

When Stars Forget to Shine

When stars forget to shine so bright,
We dance in shadows, what a sight!
With laughter echoing through the night,
We trip on dreams, oh what a flight!

The moon a witness, grinning wide,
As we embrace the cosmic ride.
With every step, oh what a glide,
In celestial corners, we confide.

Maps of Uncharted Realms

With maps drawn in crayon and cheer,
We venture forth without any fear.
Finding treasures both strange and dear,
In lands where no one will ever steer.

X marks the spot, yet we seldom see,
Where silly secrets could possibly be.
Turning over stones, just for a spree,
Discovering giggles shaped like a tree.

Embracing the Nocturnal Unknown

In the realm where shadows play,
We twirl and twine 'til break of day.
With glowing whispers leading our way,
We chase the mystery, come what may.

With owls as our raucous guides,
We bounce on dreams, like wild tides.
In darkened corners where humor hides,
We find the joy that never subsides.

Tales of the Unremarked

In corners unseen, where dust bunnies dwell,
We gather stories with a wink and a yell.
Each tale as absurd as a foghorn's swell,
Like fish riding bikes, oh can you tell?

With heroes mismatched and sidekicks bizarre,
We ride on whimsy, chasing a star.
In laughter, we find adventures afar,
While sipping our tea from a pickle jar.

Searching for Shadows

In the depths of the night,
I seek flickers of light,
But the shadows just laugh,
And tell me to take a bath.

I chase them through fields,
But laughter never yields,
For every step I take,
They giggle and just shake.

Fleeting Moments

A butterfly flaps its wings,
While I sit pondering things,
Moments vanish like smoke,
Leaving me with one joke.

I try to catch time tight,
But it dances out of sight,
Like a cat on a spree,
It just won't owe me a fee.

Endless Questions

I ask if fish can fly,
And why the moon is shy,
But logic takes a nap,
And words just form a trap.

Why do we have to try?
Is it cake or a pie?
The universe just shrugs,
While I just sip my jugs.

Emptiness Dressed in Dreams

I bought a fancy hat,
Said it would change my chat,
But it blew away fast,
Left me with dreams uncast.

I painted my hopes bright,
They vanished in the night,
Empty canvases grin,
As I look for my twin.

The Paradox of Purpose

I seek a reason bold,
With treasures yet untold,
But all I find are socks,
Hiding behind the clocks.

I ponder why we strive,
And how we stay alive,
Yet in the search for gold,
I'm caught in tales retold.

Beyond the Horizon of Hope

We seek the stars with yearning eyes,
But tripping over shoelaces, oh what a surprise!
The path is paved with riddles and jest,
Who knew confusion could be this blessed?

We plant our dreams in soil of doubt,
Watered with laughter, it's hard to shout!
But beyond the hills, the sun will gleam,
Just mind the shadows, they ruin the dream.

A Canvas Without Colors

With brushes in hand, we paint our fate,
But the colors are missing; can we still create?
Just splashes of gray on a blank, big sheet,
Art's most exciting when it's incomplete!

We frame our failures, hang them on walls,
Each stroke a giggle, with whimsical calls.
Life's masterpiece? It's a messy affair,
But who says a jigsaw can't dance in midair?

Chasing Illusions in a Silent World

We chase the shadows that play hide and seek,
Whispering nonsense when we feel weak.
Reality's laugh is a ticklish tease,
Yet we pretend that it's all meant to please.

In cafes of dreams, we sip our grins,
Trading tall tales for little wins.
But every sip's a mirage in disguise,
As the waiter grins at our surprised eyes.

Silent Songs of the Unwritten

In pages unturned, our stories wait,
With scribbled thoughts decorating fate.
But the ink spills over from laughter's pen,
Creating a symphony of whimsical men.

We hum our tunes with no notes to play,
In this orchestra of life's grand ballet.
A cacophony of chuckles fills the air,
With each note a dance—if we dare.

The Enigma of Existence

Life's a riddle, a jumbled phrase,
With missing pieces in clever ways.
We search for sense, we hunt for clues,
Yet wear mismatched socks and sing the blues.

Dance in circles, then take a nap,
Chasing shadows, left in a flap.
A punchline hidden in cosmic jest,
Laughter's our answer, so just relax and rest.

A Canvas of Chaos

Painting life with colors gone awry,
An abstract piece, just give it a try.
Brush strokes messy, a splash of fun,
Who needs Picasso when you have a pun?

Glimpses of sense in the paint so bright,
Yet all it brings is a laughing plight.
Canvas drips as we mix up our fate,
Art is subjective; let's celebrate!

Stars That Never Shine

In a cosmos where wishes go to die,
Stars flicker out, no reason why.
We'd wish on them, but they're mostly fake,
Just printouts of light for our poor hearts' ache.

Beneath this sky, we crack dumb jokes,
While pondering life with a side of hoaxes.
A galaxy of giggles, a cosmic jest,
Let's toast to the dark, we're truly blessed!

Dreams in a Fractured Reality

Waking up feels like a glitchy fight,
Where dreams collide with the blinding light.
A toaster talks while dogs recite,
Philosophy wrapped in absurdity's bite.

We chase after whispers in twisted rhyme,
Finding meaning just takes too much time.
In this cracked world, laugh at the scene,
Reality's just a poke in the screen.

Glimpses into the Abyss

Life's a circus, quite absurd,
Juggling dreams, it's all a blur.
We chase our tails, then stop and stare,
Wondering if we're really there.

Spinning wheels on crooked ground,
Trying to feel that joy we've found.
Yet here we are, a silly lot,
Asking questions that life forgot.

We paint the skies with vivid hues,
While stepping in the morning's shoes.
With logic lost and giggles near,
We toast to nonsense, laugh, and cheer!

So here's to life, that joke divine,
A riddle wrapped in silly rhyme.
We find ourselves in crazy spins,
And celebrate the absurd wins!

Patterns in the Celestial Drift

Stars dangle on a cosmic thread,
While we sit and scratch our heads.
What's this dance of fate and chance?
A wobbly leap in the cosmic trance.

Comets racing, oh such speed!
Do they know what we really need?
Galaxies twirl in a dizzy haze,
As we wander through life's odd maze.

Planets spin, or do they sway?
In the end, who's got the say?
With each sunset, a chuckle's born,
While nature whispers, "Don't you mourn!"

So let's embrace this cosmic jest,
In the chaos, we find our rest.
For laughter's light, and time's a thief,
We dance in joy, despite belief.

The Fragility of Certainty

We build our castles on shifting sand,
Holding tight to a stubborn plan.
Yet waves come crashing, oh so sly,
Laughing at our dreams to fly.

With maps in hand, we set our sails,
While life hands out its whimsical tales.
Filled with courage, we choose our way,
Then trip on life's bizarre ballet!

Certainties that once seemed grand,
Float away just like quicksand.
Yet here we stand, in playful strife,
Laughing through the dance called life!

So let's toast to plans that scatter,
And to all that doesn't really matter.
We float through doubt, we glide through fear,
Finding joy in the chaos here!

Shadows of Unseen Paths

Wanderers in a land of guesses,
We stroll through life with funny dresses.
Each turn a hop, each pause a sigh,
In shadows deep, we skim the pie.

Dodging wisdom like a game,
Giving our journeys all the blame.
Like ducks in rows, we waddle forth,
While craving bliss, and yet, more mirth.

Our feet are sore from dance and laugh,
Yet here we are, the living gaffe.
With every stumblin' step we take,
We find the joy in the big mistake!

So here's to paths where shadows play,
Where truths unfold in a funny way.
We dance through life, let the puzzlement reign,
In every twist, there's laughter again!

The Beauty of the Unresolved

In a world so full of doubt,
We chase the sun and twist about.
Answers hide like socks in drawers,
A riddle wrapped in nevermore.

With every quest for something grand,
We stumble tripping on the sand.
Life's a circus, a twist of fate,
Juggling dreams, but never late.

Expectations soaring high above,
Yet landing softly like a dove.
Truth's a jester, always sly,
Tickling hearts as moments fly.

Embrace the chaos, cheers resound,
In every folly, joy is found.
So laugh and dance, let worries free,
In life's grand play, just let it be.

Navigating the Abyss

In the depths of thought we roam,
Searching for a place called home.
Sailing ships of paper dreams,
Lost at sea of endless streams.

With each wave, a question stirs,
Why are we here, where is hers?
The stars are winks, the moon a grin,
Maybe chaos is where we win.

The compass spins, directions blur,
We navigate this life with a slur.
Each misstep is a laughter hymn,
Dancing through the fate, on a whim.

So grab an oar and paddle tight,
In this abyss, confusion's light.
With a chuckle, we ride the tide,
Together, let's enjoy the ride.

Whispers of the Unseen

In shadows deep, we hear the laugh,
Of meaning dancing on our path.
Whispers tickle, truths concealed,
A cosmic joke that won't be revealed.

The universe, a grand charade,
With every plan, a silly trade.
Like socks that vanish, where'd they go?
Life's a jest, a curious show.

With every ponder, we twist and shout,
In the puzzle, we too, flout.
Chasing tails of infinite fun,
Life's a riddle, never done.

So tune your ears to giggles low,
Seek out the joy in every flow.
For in the silence, voices sing,
Embrace the chaos, let it swing.

When Purpose Takes Flight

Purpose flaps its wings about,
Like a chicken trying to sprout.
It pecks at dreams and scratches fears,
While laughter flows like joyful tears.

Who needs a compass, maps are lame,
We'll make our own silly claim.
With every stumble, giggles bloom,
In this absurd, chaotic room.

So let's float high on whims and fancies,
Life's a dance, not all romances.
With purpose lost, let laughter win,
In joyful jest, we all begin.

Chase the flights of shimm'ring light,
In this circus of pure delight.
When purpose takes its bashful shout,
Just laugh it off, and twist about.

The Canvas of Nothingness

In a world where answers hide,
We paint with colors, oh so wide.
Yet every stroke just blends away,
A masterpiece of disarray.

We chase the sun, we chase the moon,
But life's just one big cosmic tune.
With each note played, we dance and twirl,
Then trip and fall in endless whirl.

With empty pockets, dreams we stake,
Building castles made of cake.
We sprinkle laughter, hope, and cheer,
Only to find it disappeared.

So gather 'round, and share a wink,
Life's a puzzle, what do you think?
In this grand jest, so light and free,
We find our joy in absolute glee.

Melodies of the Unheard

Whispers echo through the void,
Life's a song that's just devoid.
We hum along, not knowing why,
As tune after tune just drifts on by.

Singing loudly, shouting clear,
While no one's listening, what a fear!
Yet still we croon, with all our might,
In this grand silence, such delight.

The orchestra plays with no one there,
A symphony in thin, cold air.
Each note's a laugh, each pause a sigh,
In melodies where dreams just fly.

So take a bow, my friend, it's true,
The music flows with me and you.
In this grand farce, we take a stand,
And dance like fools, hand in hand.

The Great Cosmic Joke

Why did the stars refuse to shine?
Because they heard a punchline divine!
The universe cracks a smile so wide,
As planets laugh, and comets glide.

We plan and plot, create our fate,
But the joke's on us—it's far too late.
In tangled thoughts, we find our grace,
Playing catch with empty space.

A gravity well? A comedy show!
Chasing dreams that never grow.
The cosmic clown throws pies so sly,
While we await the big goodbye.

So here's to life, a raucous jest,
In absurdity, we find our best.
With chuckles shared and smiles wide,
We ride this wave of the cosmic tide.

Starlit Paths of the Aimless

Wandering through the glimmering night,
With no clear path, we walk in fright.
Each twinkling star a laugh, a grin,
Reflecting the chaos lurking within.

We stroll through fields of "What's the fuss?"
As if our purpose rides the bus.
But we're just here, and that's okay,
Making memories on our way.

We might trip on our own two feet,
But laughter makes our journey sweet.
In this vast dark, we find our glow,
In starlit paths where wanderers go.

So join the dance, forget the clock,
Life's a jape, it's quite the shock.
With every step, a joy defined,
In aimless strut, our hearts aligned.

A Symphony in Silence

The orchestra plays, but it's quite bare,
Not a soul is around, just the silent air.
Conductor's lost, waving his baton,
And I'm at the back, snoring along.

Jazz hands are flailing, but they lack flair,
The audience is gone, vanished in thin air.
To dance with a ghost is a peculiar sight,
But who cares? I've got snacks, and I'm feeling alright.

Searching for Stars in a Gloomy Sky

I glanced at the sky, it rained a bit,
Where are the stars? Did they throw a fit?
Moon's on a break, sipping tea on the side,
While I'm wide awake, and they're all out to hide.

Clouds told me, "Nah, it's not your night,"
"Go home, have some cake, or maybe a fright."
So I raised my cup to the absent stars,
And toasted the darkness from my favorite bars.

Epilogues of a Forgotten Dream

Once I dreamed big, oh what a sight,
But now I'm awake, and that dream took flight.
It soared like a kite on a long, windy day,
Caught in a tree, where it's bound to stay.

I searched for the dream, but it turned into fog,
Wandering around like a well-fed dog.
Finding meaning in crumbs, that's my new plan,
Till I trip on my cat, oh what a grand slam!

Beneath the Surface of Nothingness

Diving deep down where the nothingness lies,
Found a bubble of air that's covered in fries.
I swam with the fish that wore silly hats,
And had a grand time, not pondering stats.

The meaning of life? A charade on a stage,
With clowns in the spotlight, all jumping off page.
Yet here I am laughing, just floating along,
In this ocean of nonsense, where I feel I belong.

Where Thoughts Wander Aimlessly

Thoughts like balloons without a string,
Float around doing their thing.
Chasing squirrels or chasing dreams,
Who knew life was quite this strange?

Questions asked without a care,
Like lost socks in the laundry lair.
Searching meaning near a tree,
Finding none, just a bumblebee.

Laughter bubbles, life's a jest,
Finding purpose? Just take a rest.
And if you need a little more,
Join my circus, there's a door.

So here we sit, with smiles wide,
Embracing the chaos with pride.
Life's a party, come on, come on!
Let's twirl and dance till the dawn.

The Horizon of Oblivion

At the edge of the world I stand,
Gazing out at nothing planned.
A horizon that stretches so wide,
With no map, no guide, like a joyous ride.

The sun dips low, but what's the rush?
Time's a turtle, in no real crush.
Chasing shadows, playing pranks,
Wondering why we freefall in ranks.

Glimpses of past, future a blur,
Life's a puzzle, none of it sure.
So let's laugh at the cosmic show,
With popcorn in hand, let's go, let's go!

In oblivion's arms, we twirl and sway,
Nothing matters, come what may.
Grab your hats, let's take a flight,
On this endless, silly night.

Liminal Spaces of Existence

Caught between the here and there,
In a place of funny despair.
Like socks tucked under the bed,
What's the point? We giggle instead.

In waiting rooms of our own design,
We sip our coffee, perfect and fine.
Unfinished thoughts dance 'round the room,
As we ponder the next big boom.

Footsteps echo in the unknown,
In liminal spaces we've all grown.
So let's skip past the weighty stuff,
And solve this riddle of being—enough!

With a wink and a nod, let's embrace the void,
In the chaos, we find joys deployed.
Life's a joke, with punchlines a swirl,
In liminal spaces, let's give it a whirl!

The Silent Cry of a Swaying Leaf

A leaf hangs on, swaying slow,
Silent cries in the wind's flow.
"What's my purpose?" it seems to plea,
While the breeze just laughs with glee.

Dancing lightly, no care in sight,
Bouncing joyfully left and right.
What wisdom is there in falling down?
The leaf just twists, without a frown.

Moments fleeting, yet oh so bright,
In every flutter, a spark of light.
Why worry when the wind's your friend?
Swaying leaves teach—you just pretend!

So join me, leaf, let's drift on by,
In a whirl of colors, you and I.
Life's hilarious, don't you see?
Let's laugh and sway, forever free!

The Secret Life of Dust

Dust bunnies dance in the light,
Hiding secrets, out of sight.
They laugh and spin, without a care,
While the world forgets they are there.

Gathering tales from every room,
Whispers of chaos, a subtle doom.
Yet when you sweep, they swirl and flee,
Playing tag with vacuum glee.

Each speck a story, a tiny friend,
In a world where mess will never end.
They know more than we could conceive,
But don't expect them to believe.

So let them twirl, in shadow and sun,
For life's too short to just weigh a ton.
Join the dance, let laughter dust,
Embrace the nonsense, it's a must!

Dreams Written in Water

I wrote my dreams on a flowy stream,
With hopes and wishes, it seemed a dream.
But water giggled and washed them away,
Leaving me pondering the meaning of play.

Floating ideas like boats made of paper,
Sailing on currents, a slippery caper.
Each wave a laugh, a quip from the sea,
"Don't take it too serious, just let it be!"

In ripples, my thoughts dance like fish,
Chasing reflections—oh, how I wish!
But fish don't ponder, they simply swim,
While I chase shadows, it's all rather dim.

So I'll splash around, and splash some more,
In water world weirdness, what's life for?
If dreams are water, then let them flow,
In puddles of laughter, let's put on a show!

The Labyrinth of Unanswerable Questions

Why does the cat stare at the wall?
Is it pondering life, or just having a ball?
With each twist and turn in this mental maze,
I find myself lost in a perplexing haze.

Do fish get thirsty, or understand time?
Is a tree's whisper just nature's rhyme?
I ask, and the universe chuckles in glee,
As I tumble through riddles with absolute spree.

With logic, I'm building an empire of thought,
But wisdom gives way, it's all for naught.
A minotaur dances while I can't find the way,
It's rather amusing – come join the ballet!

So let's revel in questions, we'll spin and we'll swirl,
The answers are diamonds, they just make us twirl.
Inquiring minds may go quite insane,
But what is more funny than asking again?

In Search of a Fleeting Spark

I chased a spark on a windy day,
It winked at me, then danced away.
Like fireflies with a sense of sass,
Whisking me off to a jumbled morass.

With each little flicker, my hopes would rise,
But just like my socks, they vanished, oh my!
By moonlight, I searched beneath the stars,
For answers that hid in the Milky Bars.

I burned some toast, thought it was profound,
While caffeine dreams made a buzz all around.
Yet in my kitchen, through all of the fray,
A spark's just a yawn; let's forget it's my day.

So I'll gather giggles, confound all my woes,
In this grand charade where the silly wind blows.
I may never find it, that spark so divine,
But the hunt for the funny? That's perfectly fine!

Unraveled Threads of Existence

In a world of knots and strings,
We search for meaning while chaos sings.
Tangled thoughts in a jumbled dance,
Life's a joke, and we're caught by chance.

We chase bright stars on a cloudy night,
But find lost socks, oh what a plight!
Existence is like a game gone wrong,
Where nothing fits and we all play along.

The search for sense is a wild spree,
Like trying to make sense of a bumblebee.
Laughing through tears and upside-down fates,
We toast to confusion and double dates.

So here's to the fun in our goofy ride,
With laughter and blunders, we'll take it in stride.
Embrace the absurd, it's quite a delight,
In this riddle called life, there's no end in sight.

Dancing in the Absurd

Life's a waltz with two left feet,
We tumble and twirl, oh isn't it sweet!
With every misstep, we burst out in giggles,
Embracing the chaos as it wiggles.

The universe laughs at our silly ways,
We throw confetti on convoluted days.
In a dance of madness, we find our place,
Two clowns on the stage, with paint-splashed face.

We spin in circles, looking for signs,
Chasing shadows of meant-to-be lines.
Yet in this folly, we find our cheer,
Shaking our heads at the lack of a steer.

So let's shake our hips to this cosmic jest,
In the theater of life, we're all guests.
With laughter as music, we'll spin till we drop,
In the wacky world of a never-ending hop.

The Mirage of Certainty

We build thick walls of 'should' and 'must',
Only to realize they crumble to dust.
With every grand plan leading to fluff,
We question if certainty's just a bluff.

Expectations loom like shadows of dread,
But curveballs fly through our dreams instead.
Life's a magic show, smoke and mirrors,
With laughter our armor against all the fears.

Finding some logic is like chasing air,
We attempt to capture the seemingly rare.
Yet in the confusion, a spark starts to glow,
It's funnier still when we just let it flow.

So let's toast to questions without clear reply,
With a wink and a nod, we'll give it a try.
In the land of the unsure, let's spin and prance,
For life is the punchline in this wild dance.

Wanderers in the Infinite

We're aimless drifters on this great sphere,
Searching for wisdom, yet drawing near fear.
With backpacks of dreams and snacks made of hope,
We wander the paths, fitting in with the slope.

Each twist and turn leads us round and round,
Chasing the echoes of a lost sound.
With giggles and questions like balloons in the air,
We float through the madness, not a single care.

In a universe vast, still we hold hands,
Jumping through hoops with no set plans.
In laughter, we find something quite profound,
That life's greatest treasures are rarely found.

So here's to the wanderers, brave and absurd,
In the cosmic carnival, we're never deterred.
With hearts full of joy and heads in the stars,
We'll dance to our rhythm, no matter how far.

Fables of the Unheard

In a land where chickens roam,
A snail built a mobile home.
He said with pride, "I'm quite the catch,"
While speeding past a sleeping patch.

The cows held court, debated fate,
While pigeons plotted to innovate.
Straws in hats declared the day,
A harvest feast of words to play.

Yet somewhere deep in the fields,
A cat dreamed dreams of wondrous yields.
He licked his paws, so wise and sly,
While wondering why the sky was dry.

The tales of critters, loud and proud,
Brought laughter to the wandering crowd.
In fables sung with utmost cheer,
Who needs a meaning when fun is near?

Beneath the Stars

Beneath the stars, the crickets chirp,
Comparing goals and feeling burped.
A raccoon claimed he held the key,
To unlock life's sweet mystery.

The moon just laughed, with shining glee,
You'd think it knew the latest spree.
A cat sprawled out to soak the light,
As if to say, "Hey, this feels right!"

A frog croaked loud, "Let's make a deal,"
"We'll trade our woes for a happy meal!"
The owl just hooted, wise and old,
While wishing he was brave and bold.

So dance among the twinkling skies,
With bright ideas and silly highs.
For in this world of joy and jest,
The cosmos holds no need for quest.

Alone

Alone on a couch, a potato's plight,
He dreams of chips 'neath the TV light.
With a remote in hand, he declares,
"Life's true magic is cooking chairs!"

The fridge hums tunes of frozen dreams,
While spoons plot culinary schemes.
Suddenly, the toast starts to chat,
Stating proudly, "I'm the real diplomat!"

In this solo dance of crumbs and whims,
The walls join in with silly hymns.
A jar of pickles gives a shout,
"Who needs a meaning? Let's just spout!"

So here's to those who sit and grin,
Finding joy in the quirky din.
For solitude can bring delight,
As laughter echoes through the night.

Codes of the Unwritten

In the forest of dreams, a squirrel pranced,
With acorns on his head, he danced.
He scribbled codes upon a bark,
Of secret snacks after dark.

The owls discussed the bookless lore,
While rabbits debated an open door.
"Why think too hard?" a crow said, sly,
"Just wing it all and say goodbye!"

In fields of wheat, a scarecrow hummed,
As corn stalks joined in the beat, they bummed.
With whispers shared, the crows took flight,
In search of feasts under the moonlight.

So laugh along with nature's craze,
Forget the rules, embrace the maze.
For in the whimsy of unsung words,
Life writes its own tune, it's absurd!

Echoes Through Empty Halls

In a castle made of cardboard dreams,
Echoes waltzed through the silent beams.
A ghost jested, 'I'm here for fun,'
While counting dust, "I've got no gun."

The chandeliers swung with clarion calls,
As mice debated the best of balls.
In gowns of cheese, they twirled with glee,
Who needs a meaning when just to be?

The echoes resonated with quirky tunes,
A melody danced beneath the moons.
Spirits chuckled, "This life's a game,"
Reveling here, with no one to blame.

So let the laughter fill the halls,
In this merry land where nothing falls.
For joy is found in every crack,
In echoes of life, there's nothing lacked.

Images of Impermanence

Clouds dance by, shaped like a cow,
As I ponder why I can't see how.
A fleeting thought, like a butterfly's flight,
Fading too quick, lost to the night.

The grass is green, or so I've been told,
But even it wilts, as the seasons grow old.
A smile for a moment, a fleeting grin,
Life's just a show where we can't seem to win.

We cling to moments, yet slip through our hands,
Like sandcastles built on the shifting sands.
Laughter and tears, they come and they go,
A never-ending circus, featuring the show.

And so we march on, a merry old crew,
In this bizarre dance, what else can we do?
The stage is set, let the farce now unfold,
For in this hilarity, we find laughs untold.

Tides of the Unfathomable

Waves crash down, like my hopes every day,
The ocean giggles, then carries them away.
I sit on the shore, munching fries from a cart,
While pondering the nature of my very own heart.

The moon pulls strings, like a puppeteer,
Yet my life's just a mess, let's be clear.
I laugh at the nonsense, my fate's a big joke,
With fortune cookies, but no fortune to poke.

The tide rolls in, and my worries all fade,
Like socks in the dryer, where they lie unmade.
I dip my toes in, let the water tickle,
And ponder the point of this endless little riddle.

So let's ride the waves, or at least watch them crash,
In this salty ballet of life's futile splash.
With a side of chuckles, let chaos abide,
For finding our way, I'll just go for the ride.

Chronicles of the Inconsequential

Once upon a time in a world oh-so-small,
A bug crawled by, didn't care at all.
I waved hello, but it just wiggled tight,
Ignoring my charm in the fading daylight.

A pebble once rolled, it had dreams to be grand,
But it just sat back, on the soft, golden sand.
With a sigh of relief, I gave it a name,
But did it matter? It's still just the same.

A paper airplane could soar through the skies,
Yet here I am, stuck, with my mundane sighs.
It lands with a thump, not a hero's decree,
Just a tale of a flutter, no great mystery.

So let's write our stories, let whimsy take flight,
For in a world of nonsense, we'll just hold on tight.
With laughter as armor, we'll bravely engage,
In the chronicles penned on an inconsequential page.

The Fabric of Lost Dreams

We stitched our desires in colors so bright,
But life turned the canvas to shades of twilight.
Each pixel a promise that faded with glee,
As we chased after yarns that unraveled with me.

Once, I dreamed of castles, now threads filled with fluff,
The fabric a tapestry, but oh, so tough!
I weave my ambitions with laughter and thread,
But sometimes it feels like I'm stuck in my bed.

A patchwork of wishes, oh what a delight,
I wore them like armor, yet lost the fight.
The seams may unravel, but humor's my seam,
Stitched up with giggles, I'm still chasing that dream.

So gather the scraps of what used to be gold,
In this crazy cocoon, I'm still feeling bold.
With needles of wit, let me stitch up my fate,
In the fabric of laughter, I'll celebrate.

Stars That Fade at Dawn

In the sky, we chase bright lights,
Wishing well on moonlit nights.
But morning comes, they all take flight,
Leaving us with thoughts of bite.

We dance with dreams, a silly waltz,
Pretend to make no single fault.
Yet, as we trip, we laugh and cheer,
Knowing reason's just a smear.

Life's a game of tag, my friend,
We run in circles, never end.
Chasing shadows, losing ground,
In the laughter, joy is found.

So raise a glass to fleeting stars,
To dreams on hold, and silly cars.
We'll play the fools, oh can't you see,
In this circus, we're all free!

Melodies of the Unattainable

A tune we hum but cannot hear,
Chasing notes that disappear.
Dancing to a silent song,
Wondering why we sing along.

We pluck the strings of empty hope,
In a room without a scope.
The band plays on, the crowd looks grand,
But none can find a steady hand.

With every verse, we lose our way,
A symphony of shades of gray.
And yet, we twirl without a care,
In a concert of the unaware.

So raise your voice if you can't sing,
Join the chaos, let the bells ring!
For in the laughter, in the fun,
We find our rhythm, everyone.

The Paradox of Seeking

We hunt for gold in fields of hay,
Digging deep on a sunny day.
But what is found, we soon forget,
Just another day in our silly net.

Questions dance, they twist and flip,
On this absurd yet joyful trip.
With all the answers out of sight,
We ponder on with all our might.

The search feels real, yet silly too,
We're lost in riddles through and through.
It's all a joke, a jester's game,
A carnival of thoughts to tame.

So lift your glass and toast with glee,
To seeking what can never be!
In this folly, we find delight,
A paradox that feels just right.

All Roads Lead to Nowhere

We wander paths with signs unclear,
Thinking each turn brings us near.
But every route just fizzles away,
In a swirl of dust, come what may.

On each road, a tale unfolds,
Of dreams that we were never told.
Yet laughing loud, we press on still,
In our absurd, yet charming thrill.

With maps that lead to coffee shops,
We'll gather 'round and share the flops.
In every bump, there's joy to find,
As life's a ride for the light-hearted mind.

So here's to detours, roads galore,
To every stop, we drink and snore!
For in this traveling, wild and free,
We pen our story, you and me.

The Illusion of Certainty

In a world where answers tease,
We search for clues like lost car keys.
The signs we follow often mislead,
Yet still, we march, a comical breed.

We build our castles in shifting sand,
With blueprints written by a shaky hand.
Certainty's a jester, cracking smiles,
While we juggle life's chaotic trials.

Dreams of fortune dance in our heads,
But our plans just end up like tangled threads.
As we laugh at fate's absurd design,
We raise a toast with our plastic wine.

So here's to hopes that float like foam,
And questions that wander far from home.
In this circus of jest, we take our seat,
Life's punchline's here, not so discreet.

Chasing Shadows at Dusk

As the sun dips low, we roam the dark,
Pursuing dreams like a curious lark.
With shadows as companions, we sashay along,
In this dance of the silly, we all belong.

A butterfly flutters, it's a fleeting chase,
Life's a game of tag in a silly space.
We chase our tails, and the moon just grins,
While reality winks, wearing silly pins.

The echoes of laughter collide with the night,
As we search for wisdom within our delight.
Grasping at wisps of elusive air,
Finding meaning in moments, if none's really there.

So waltz with me in this twilight glow,
Where shadows are friends, and laughter flows.
For who needs the answers? Let's play in the mist,
We're all just shadows, how could we resist?

When Questions Outnumber Answers

We scribble our queries on napkins and walls,
With hopes that the universe gently calls.
Yet more questions sprout like weeds in the sun,
As we ponder the meaning of having fun.

Why is it always one step ahead?
Every answer feels like just another thread.
With doubt as our compass, we wander and roam,
Searching for sense in the chaos we comb.

So how can we win when it's rigged from the start?
With a jester's grin, life plays its part.
For every solution we think we've found,
Like smoke in the wind, it dances around.

Thus, let's toast to the bliss of the vague,
Where questions amuse like a playful plague.
In this circus of life, with its riddle of fate,
We laugh at the chaos; it's never too late.

Echoes of a Silent Anthem

In a world that sings without a tune,
We sway like leaves under a balloon.
The anthem of silence can be so loud,
As we gather confusion in a whimsical crowd.

We march to the beat of a nonsensical drum,
In the land of what-ifs, we all become numb.
With banners of laughter, we dance along,
In this silent chorus, we all belong.

Melodies of mischief paint the day bright,
As the curious stumble into the night.
Our hearts beat in rhythm with quirky delight,
In this echo chamber, we savor the light.

From questions unanswered, we spin our tale,
With a wink and a smile, we set our sail.
In the absurdity's glow, let's raise our cheer,
For the echoes of laughter are all that we hear.

Ephemeral Whispers

In a world of fleeting dreams,
We chase the glitter, or so it seems.
With hugs from clouds and kisses from rain,
We laugh at our folly, then do it again.

The sun's just an actor on a big stage bright,
Performing its role in a cosmic light.
But when the curtain falls, does it all fade?
Cue the crickets, oh what a charade!

Fading Shadows of Purpose

Life's like a burrito, wrapped up tight,
Filled with wisdom—or maybe just spite.
As we munch through existence, spoon in hand,
We ponder if nachos should've been planned.

With puzzles unsolved and maps upside down,
We search for the meaning in this big town.
But the street signs are broken, the compass spins,
Just grab a taco; let's see where it wins!

Emptiness in Bloom

A flower bloomed where nothing should grow,
It laughed yet felt empty—it stole the show.
With petals that giggled and roots that sighed,
It wondered why life had to be so wide.

The bees made their visits, all busy and bright,
While the flower just thought, 'Is this really right?'
So it danced with the breeze, turned to the sky,
Wishing to know why the clouds drifted by.

The Maze of Existence

We wander through mazes of life with zeal,
Where lost is the new name for the real deal.
With each twist and turn, a giggle escapes,
As we bump into walls wearing muffin capes.

Meet the sage with his riddles in tow,
He says, 'What's the point?' as he nibbles on dough.
Existence feels like a game of charades,
Teasing out answers like some grand parade.

A Planet Adrift in Space

In cosmos vast with stars so bright,
A planet spins on late at night.
It wonders if it's lost for good,
While critters dance like no one should.

With aliens who cook a stew,
Debating skies of purple hue.
They laugh and joke, in zero G,
About the lack of destiny.

A comet zooms, they wave hello,
While pondering what they don't know.
The vacuum holds no grand design,
Yet still, they sip their jello wine.

So here we float, no chart, no map,
In space's endless, funny gap.
With giggles echoing through the void,
Life's meaning? A cosmic ploy enjoyed!

Colors of a Fleeting Moment

A splash of yellow, a wink of red,
Life's but a canvas; colors spread.
We paint our woes with shades so bright,
Then laugh at smears in morning light.

Blue skies remind us of our dreams,
While green grass teases with its beams.
Yet moments fade, and brushes dry,
What's left behind? Just a big sigh.

With whimsy swirling like a dance,
We grasp at meaning, given a chance.
But tangled up in hues we find,
Our palette's just a state of mind.

So mix the paints and spill 'em wide,
In life's grand art, just take a ride.
If all's a joke, then let it be,
A fleeting moment - wild and free!

Dances of Chance

Two socks in laundry, one stands alone,
While others twist in a swirling drone.
They giggle at the chance of fate,
In this odd dance, they celebrate.

A tumbleweed rolls through the scene,
Flirting with clouds, a wanderer keen.
It whispers secrets, no one can hear,
While squirrels giggle, sipping beer.

The dice get thrown, the cards are played,
Life's a gamble, not a charade.
With a wink and nudge, we roll on through,
What will we win? Nobody knew!

So spin the wheel, let laughter ring,
In this grand show, we're all the bling.
With every twist, a chance to prance,
So enjoy the steps of this haphazard dance!

The Parable of the Unnoticed

A pebble sits upon the trail,
It dreams of being a boat or whale.
Yet no one sees its hopeful gleam,
In the grand ol' world, it's just a meme.

A tree grows tall with leaves so green,
Yet whispers secrets, soft and keen.
It laughs at birds and all their fuss,
For in its rings, life's hidden plus.

With ants that march in tidy rows,
They plot and scheme, or so it goes.
Yet when they stop, they share a thought,
To them, the world is never caught.

So let us pause, look twice or thrice,
For life's the spice in plain disguise.
And in the mundane, joy's keen delight,
In the unnoticed, we find our light!

Eclipsed by Reality

The sun's a soft cheese, they say,
But life does not care, it slips away.
Chasing bright stars in a cardboard box,
While truth does the twist, it always mocks.

We laugh in the face of gray, dreary days,
Searching for meaning in peculiar ways.
Glimmers of hope spark like fireflies bright,
Yet darkness wins out; it's quite the delight.

The Puzzle Without Pieces

A jigsaw with holes, it makes no sense,
Each corner and edge pays no recompense.
We gather the fragments, we search for the light,
But the picture we yield is quite a poor sight.

We laugh at the chaos, embrace the absurd,
In a world that's confused, truth's barely heard.
So grab a slice of cake, let foolishness reign,
For sanity's long gone, dancing in the rain.

Reflections in a Dreamless Mirror

Mirrors can lie, or maybe they jest,
Reflecting our dreams at their very best.
With each fleeting glance, what do we perceive?
A winking facade that yells, "Just believe!"

We twirl and we spin, with laughter we're clad,
Life's just a joke—oh isn't it mad?
In empty reflections, we paint with a grin,
For truth is a riddle we're destined to spin.

Knots in the Fabric of Time

Time's tangled yarn is quite the delight,
Each twist and each turn adds to our plight.
We stitch and we seam with a giggle and sigh,
While questions arise, like confetti they fly.

So hold tight your socks and enjoy the parade,
As reason takes flight, and logic does fade.
In knots we do dance, with a laugh that won't stop,
For life's just a circus, and we're all in the shop.

The End of the Road to Meaning

I searched for meaning in my shoe,
But all I found was a sticky goo.
So I turned around, went back to bed,
Convinced that comfort rests my head.

With coffee stains and crumbs galore,
I pondered life while on the floor.
A meme or two, and I was fine,
Who needs deep thoughts? I'll sip my wine.

The clock ticks on, I vacuum dreams,
Life's not a puzzle, it's just seams.
If laughter's gold, then I'm the king,
At least I found joy in wobbling.

So goodbye quest for wisdom's light,
I'll make silly faces all night.
The road to meaning's a looping loop,
Join me in this ridiculous group!

Ripples in Still Water

A pebble dropped, it sparked a thought,
Does life mean more than what I've bought?
I giggled hard, then spilled my drink,
The answer's clearer than I think.

In still water, thoughts start to swirl,
With giggles bubbling, and dreams that twirl.
The ducks just quack, and wander near,
Even they don't seem to care, I fear.

So let's skip stones and make a mess,
Forget the weight of life's excess.
In ripples, I find joy anew,
Mud on my shoes means life's a zoo!

Now I embrace the splashes right,
Dance in the puddles, laugh in delight.
For life's a giggle, not a drag,
Wear silly hats and waggish swag!

Shadows of Forgotten Aspirations

In corners dark, they like to hide,
My dreams of fame, and all that pride.
But shadows dance with laughter bright,
Reminding me I'm a silly sight.

A job well done? An empty quest,
My talents bloom in simple jest.
With chicken dance and quirky pose,
I redefine what greatness knows.

Forgotten goals, like socks in piles,
They laugh at me with cheeky smiles.
So I embrace my whimsy's flow,
Who knew success was just for show?

Oh shadows, keep your lighthearted tease,
For I will sprout my roots with ease.
Let laughter guide my awkward dreams,
In silly moments, life redeems!

Threads of an Unwritten Tale

I pick up threads, they swirl and weave,
Each tangled mess, I can't believe.
This story's wild, with laughs so free,
Why plot it out? Let's just be free!

With scribbles here and doodles there,
My plot unravels, but who would care?
With snacks in hand and quirky style,
I draw my life—a comic smile.

Each line a giggle, every page a jest,
Why write the rules? Let's just be blessed.
In chaos, I find my little glee,
So grab your pens! Let's be carefree!

Tickling tales in playful arcs,
Waiting for laughs, like jumping sparks.
Let's weave our lives in hues so bright,
For in our madness, we find delight!

The Weight of Lightness

We float like feathers, so carefree,
Giggling at gravity, you and me.
Life's a joke, a cosmic jest,
Searching for meaning in a lost quest.

With every leap, our worries fade,
Dancing on clouds, unafraid.
Who needs a map or a guiding star?
Just spin in circles, that's who we are.

The weight of lightness, oh what a dream,
Life's just a part of a larger scheme.
Like clowns in a circus, we play our role,
Laughing and prancing without a goal.

So, take my hand, let's skip and hop,
At the top of the world, we'll never stop.
For in this madness, let joy ignite,
In the absurdity, we find our light.

Silence Speaks of the Unsaid

In silence there's giggles, hidden laughter,
Whispers of nonsense, ever after.
The unspoken thoughts, a merry dance,
Like socks on a cat, a silly chance.

Words often stumble, take a vacation,
Leaving us awkward in conversation.
We nod and grin, eyes all aglow,
Debating if bananas are green or yellow.

So let's embrace the moments we freeze,
With chuckles and grins, put souls at ease.
The unsaid speaks louder, oh what a find,
Life's funny puzzle, just blow your mind.

In the void where chatters seem to fumble,
Laughter whispers softly, never grumble.
For the best joked punchline is yet to play,
In silence we find our goofy way.

Winds of Uncertainty

The winds blow wildly, a gust of surprise,
Twirling our thoughts like leaves to the skies.
With every stumble, we dance out of tune,
Bopping along to a whimsical tune.

Questions parade, a comical sight,
Yet answers are scarce, try as we might.
Like socks in the dryer, they twist and they twirl,
Finding the logic in this mad swirl.

So raise your glass to the winds unknown,
Cheers to the chaos, let it be shown.
Jump on the breeze, let it carry you high,
For in playful uncertainty, we learn to fly.

We'll laugh at the storms, and run in the rain,
Embracing the weirdness, dodging the mundane.
For life's just a kite, flying through strife,
Unraveled yet free, in the winds of life.

Footprints in the Sand of Time

We leave our marks on this sandy shore,
Tiny impressions, they mean so much more.
With each step we take, a giggle escapes,
Tracing the tides while wearing fun shapes.

Waves laugh and crash, erasing our trails,
A reminder that life's just whimsical tales.
Footprints may vanish, but still we play,
In the grand ocean, let's splash away.

So collect all your giggles, toss them like shells,
Share them with dolphins, oh, how it swells!
The sands of our stories may shift and slide,
But joy is the treasure that we cannot hide.

Dance in the sunlight, skip without care,
For in every moment, there's joy to declare.
Life's but a grain, yet oh so divine,
In the footprints of laughter, together, we shine.

Paradoxes in the Twilight

In shadows where the answers hide,
Cats chase tails, yet never abide.
Tick-tock sings the clock's mad cheer,
While time itself just disappears.

We juggle thoughts in empty air,
Clowns on unicorns, unaware.
The wise man laughs with tales to spin,
But finds the humor deep within.

We build our towers, high and grand,
With blocks of dreams, like grains of sand.
Yet each sunrise brings a jest,
As meaning checks out, a curious guest.

In twilight's glow, we spin and twist,
Searching for purpose we can't resist.
But life's a riddle, jesters feign,
That laughter echoes, sweetly insane.

Laughter in the Void

In the void, where silence reigns,
A chorus of giggles breaks the chains.
Stars twinkle gently, but who can tell,
If they're winking or caught in a spell?

The universe burps in cosmic glee,
As planets wobble, just like me.
Black holes grin, devouring light,
While I ponder my next meal tonight.

Life flips pancakes in shades of gray,
Each one a riddle that's here to play.
We dance with shadows, laugh at the steep,
Finding the humor in just being cheap.

With every tick, the absurd enhances,
While gravity pulls us into our chances.
So let's toast to nothing, raise a glass,
In the void's embrace, our doubts surpass.

A Dance with Destiny's Ghost

With ghosts that dance in polka dots,
We stumble through life, all tied up in knots.
Destiny's giggles, a mischievous sprite,
Pulling our strings, day and night.

We twirl and trip, on purpose we glide,
Chasing our tails with nothing to hide.
Fate's sense of humor, a playful delight,
Bends all the rules, oh what a sight!

Each misstep echoes in silent halls,
Like marionettes with invisible thralls.
But laughter resounds in a soft, sweet refrain,
Turning our stumbles into a game.

So waltz with the ghost, don't take it too hard,
Life's just a dance, with laughter as guard.
In every slip, find the jester's role,
Embrace the absurd, and give it your soul.

Unraveled Threads of Being

In fabric spun from the threads of fate,
We knit our dreams with a touch of debate.
But lo and behold, they tangle and fray,
As life's needle works in a mischievous way.

Unraveled thoughts scatter like leaves,
While logic teases, and common sense grieves.
We wear masks of wisdom, but underneath,
A clown hearts our essence, spreading mirthlike a wreath.

Socks missing pairs in the laundry of time,
We chase after sense, but it's just a rhyme.
These threads may form tapestries grand,
Yet laughter remains the warmest strand.

So snicker at patterns that come undone,
For life's a tapestry meant to be fun.
We patch it with joy, in every seam,
Finding meaning in the chaos, it seems.

A Puzzle with Missing Pieces

Life's a jigsaw, all a blur,
Pieces that just won't concur.
I found a corner, no edge in sight,
Maybe it's art? Oh, what a fright!

Cats steal pieces, kids scream in glee,
Searching for answers that won't set us free.
Count all your blessings, well... if you can,
Maybe it's just a cosmic prank on man!

Every box claims it's a full set,
Yet I still find stones where I once had fret.
But it's all in good fun, don't shed a tear,
Just grab a soda and laugh at the sheer!

When life's a puzzle with missing parts,
Embrace the chaos, it's where fun starts.
Savor the nonsense, let giggles unfold,
In this grand riddle, life won't be sold!

The Heartbeat of the Unresolved

Tick-tock goes the clock, but what's the rush?
Questions parade, like an awkward crush.
What's it all for? Who even knows?
At least we've got snacks—hey, look, some prose!

Life's like a movie with no clear script,
Every twist lands with a belly-flop dip.
So let's dance in circles, turn up the cheer,
The unresolved squeaks, but hey, we're still here!

Romance mingles with existential dread,
But a good laugh can lift your head.
Let's not decipher this maddening tale,
Popcorn and punchlines will always prevail!

So let's toast to the questions, health to the flops,
And remember: punchlines can sometimes be props.
In the heartbeat of chaos, what a grand show,
Life's quirks in abundance, just watch as we go!

A Song Without Lyrics

Whistling tunes without a clue,
Singing from hearts, but missing a view.
Ode to confusion, a chuckle or two,
Let's strum the nonsense until it's true!

Notes dance around like they lost their way,
A catchy refrain, but what did it say?
Life's a melody that skips on the beat,
Just hum along and don't feel defeat!

Banjos and flutes in a chaotic blend,
Can't find the chorus, but who needs a friend?
Just laugh at the silence, join in the strife,
For we all echo this wacky ol' life!

So grab your old kazoo, let's make a scene,
Life's a jam session, outrageous and keen.
A song without lyrics, free as the breeze,
Let laughter be music, and dance as you please!

Whims of the Ineffable

Waves crash softly on the beach of thought,
Where questions bubble with answers sought.
But the tide pulls back, leaving sand so bare,
What whimsical nonsense lies dancing in air?

Mystics scribble on napkins with flair,
But even they trip on the cosmic affair.
A gorilla in sunglasses and bells has a say,
"Maybe just laugh at the chaos, okay?"

Life's just a circus, no knots to untie,
clowns in the spotlight, juggling the sky.
When clarity eludes, create your own fun,
A waltz of the baffled, we dance 'til we're done!

So embrace the absurd, in this masquerade,
With whimsy in pockets, we'll dance unafraid.
The ineffable whispers, as we grin and sway,
Life's just a giggle, come join in the play!

www.ingramcontent.com/pod-product-compliance
Lightning Source LLC
Chambersburg PA
CBHW051701160426
43209CB00004B/982